White Wine

André Dominé

White Wine

Photography
Armin Faber
Thomas Pothmann

Feierabend

© 2003 Feierabend Verlag OHG
Mommsenstraße 43
D-10629 Berlin

Project Management: Bettina Freeman
Translation from German: Mariana Schroeder
Editing: Lizzie Gilbert
Typesetting: Roman Bold & Black, Cologne
Design: Sonja Loy, Cologne
Lithography: Kölnermedienfabrik, Cologne
Printing and Binding: Christians Druckerei GmbH & Co. KG, Hamburg

Printed in Germany

ISBN 3-936761-54-x
61-04002-1

Contents

France

Switzerland

Germany

Italy

Spain

A Glanc

stralia

ROSEMOUNT
ESTATE

ROXBURGH

HUNTER VALLEY

LINDEMANS
BIN 65
CHARDONNAY
1996

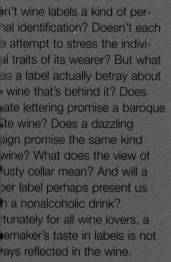

YARRA RIDGE

999 YARRA VALLEY
AUVIGNON BLANC
PRODUCED BY YARRA RIDGE VINEYARD
YARRA GLEN VICTORIA
PRODUCT OF AUSTRALIA 750ml

New Zealand

CLOUDY BAY

SAUVIGNON BLANC 1999

U.S.A.

RED SHOULDER RANCH

Shafer

1998
Napa Valley
Carneros

CHARDONNAY

Grown, Produced & Bottled by
Shafer Vineyards, Napa, CA
Alcohol 14.5% by Volume

ALBAN VINEYARDS

VIOGNIER
Edna Valley 1996
ALBAN ESTATE VINEYARD

A Syrah Worth
Fighting Over?

You Bet Shiraz!

EBERLE

A Pioneer of California Syrah.
Extremely Limited.
Extremely Good.

EVESHAM
WOOD
Le Puits Sec
19 99
Pinot Gris
WILLAMETTE VALLEY APPELLATION

Hanzell
SONOMA VALLEY
CHARDONNAY

HANZELL VINEYARDS, SONOMA, CALIFORNIA

COLUMBIA VALLEY
LATE HARVEST
SEMILLON

Chateau Ste Michelle

Argentina

MENDOZA

Luigi Bosca

RIESLING
1997

Chile

MONTES ALPHA
Chardonnay
1997

to the **World** of **White Wine**

SANTA CAROLINA
SAUVIGNON BLANC
1999

n't wine labels a kind of per-
nal identification? Doesn't each
e attempt to stress the indivi-
al traits of its wearer? But what
es a label actually betray about
wine that's behind it? Does
ate lettering promise a baroque
te wine? Does a dazzling
sign promise the same kind
wine? What does the view of
usty cellar mean? And will a
er label perhaps present us
h a nonalcoholic drink?
tunately for all wine lovers, a
emaker's taste in labels is not
ays reflected in the wine.

Austria

NOUVELLE VAGUE
1996

WEINLAUBENHOF

KRACHER

BURGENLAND

GRANDE CUVÉE
TROCKENBEEREN-
AUSLESE

NUMMER

7

Süss-alc. 12,5% vol
375 ML
Erzeugerabfüllung:
Prädikatswein "L"-E 9051/98
Kracher - A-7142 Illmitz

ÖSTERREICH · NEUSIEDLERSEE

Weingut
PEILER-ARTINGER

1996
RUSTER AUSBRUCH
NEUSIEDLERSEE-HÜGELLAND
ÖSTERREICH

ERZEUGERABFÜLLUNG
A-7071 RUST, HAUPTSTRASSE 3, TEL. 0 26 85 / 227
PRÄDIKATSWEIN LE 600497   SÜSS
13,5% vol   0,375 l

WIENINGER

CHARDONNAY
1996
- Grand Select -

WIENER WEIN

Hungary

Sämling 88

Trockenbeeren-
alc. 8,5% vol
auslese 1995
süß

Lang

Weingut
Helmut
Lang
A-7142 ILLMITZ
Quergasse 5
☎ & Fax 02175/2923

Neusiedlersee · Österreich
Erzeugerabfüllung
Prädikatswein "L" E 8280/96   € 0,375 l

CHATEAU PAJZOS
TOKAJI

South Africa

Chardonnay
Wine of Origin Overberg

EST. 1896

Paul Cluver
Sauvignon Blanc
1998

ESTATE WINE OF ORIGIN-ELGIN
PRODUCT OF THE REPUBLIC OF SOUTH AFRICA

GROOT CONSTANTIA
ESTATE WINE

WYN VAN OORSPRONG CONSTANTIA

SAUVIGNON BLANC
VINTAGE 1998 DESKAAR

GEKWEEK GEMAAK EN GEBOTTEL OP GROOT
CONSTANTIA LANDGOED

750ml   13,5% VOL
PRODUCED AND BOTTLED IN THE REPUBLIC OF SOUTH AFRICA   A332

Nothing is possible without the nose, neither above nor inside the glass. Thanks to our nose, we can enjoy the extremely complex scent of wine and therefore discover its "nose."

WHITE

White wines er through an abu dance of flavors reminiscent of flowers and her fruits and delic spices. Let you be surprised ar at times aston- ished. Have fur with wine!

DELIGHT

Sometimes sparkling and boisterous, sometimes lingering, even mysterious – then exciting, cheerful, making you laugh. Does all this really stem from white wine? Who knows – the main thing is that you share the enjoyment.

Throughout the oeuvre of Johann Wolfgang von Goethe, there are several allusions to his love of white wine. In his *West-Eastern Divan,* published in 1819, he compares drunkenness caused by wine with love, stating that both inspire him. But while the drunkenness caused by wine leaves as soon as morning dawns, that feeling of drunkenness caused by love haunts him day and night and inspires him to write his songs and poems. To Goethe, this feeling of drunkenness, be it caused by love, poetry or wine, is a divine state of mind even if it means as much torment as delight.

Fans of White Wine

Goethe

While Johann Wolfgang von Goethe was writing his *West-Eastern Divan* in the garden of the Brentano family in the Rheingau-area, he praised the local wine made from selected grapes *(Trockenbeerenauslese)*, calling it the "Finger of God". Goethe was an enthusiastic white wine drinker and especially loved the wine from Würzburg. In 1806 he wrote to his wife from Jena, "Send me some more bottles of Würzburger because no other wine tastes as good to me, and I get morose when my favorite drink runs out." He must have consumed considerable quantities: When he took the waters at Carlsbad, he tried to limit his consumption, promising not to drink more than two liters per day. In general, he valued good food and drink and preferred local to international specialties. There is poetry and truth in white wine – not only for Goethe. Many men of letters like Walther von der Vogelweide, Voltaire, Friedrich Schiller, Clemens Brentano, and Gottfried Keller preferred white wine served as *Schoppen,* ¼ l helpings. Among those statesmen who were also avid white wine drinkers are Prince Metternich, Henry IV and Charlemagne.

Charlemagne

The emperor of the Holy Roman Empire was anything but an enthusiastic drinker. Although he partook of wine only moderately and loathed drunkenness in his immediate surroundings, he loved wine and supported the planting of grapevines. When he noticed, while sailing on the Rhine, that the snow on the Johannisberg hillside had melted earlier than elsewhere, he ordered vine shoots to be planted there. On a journey through Burgundy, the Montagne de Corton attracted his attention. There too, vine shoots were planted at his command – white wine grapes, because red wine would have dyed his beard. In 775 he bequeathed this vineyard to the Abbey of Saulieu, keeping the wine from the best plots for his own use. To this day this special location bears the name *Corton-Charlemagne*.

Henry IV

When the future King Henry IV was born on December 13, 1553, his grandfather Henry d'Albret, ruler of Navarre, moistened the infant's lips first with the sweet white wine Jurançon and then rubbed them with garlic. Thus he assured that the future king would begin his life with the right taste. According to legend, Henry remained true to the hearty specialties of his native Béarn throughout his life. Admittedly he also acquired a taste for the red Burgundies from Givry and even declared that the wine grown in Paris was healthy, but he enjoyed no wine more than Jurançon. Since he was often threatened by assassins, his cupbearer was ordered to sample the wine. Once, when he forgot himself and emptied the goblet with pleasure, the King remarked dryly, "Hey brother! At least you could have drunk to my health."

The Love of Wine

Not seldom does a life-long love of wine begin on a sunny summer day with a glass of cool white wine. It sparkles, it is clear and inviting. Its scent of flowers, pomes or citrus fruit like lemon or grapefruit awakens the desire to savor it. And the fresh, lively, fruity taste is seldom disappointing. You are seduced before you know why.

The White Paradox

Regular but moderate consumption of red wine diminishes the risk of heart attack, even when you like eating well. Thanks to this phenomenon, known as the "French Paradox", it is possible to be both a health fanatic and a habitual red wine drinker. So what about white wine? Fortunately, it also has its qualities. Admittedly it lacks the antioxidant, *polyphenol,* but through moderate daily consumption, it is possible to reduce health hazards just the same. *Ethanol* plays a positive role along with vitamins, minerals and trace elements contained in wine. They improve the blood fat level by sinking LDL cholesterol deposits in blood vessels. Enjoyment of white wine also has a beneficial effect on HDL cholesterol. Moreover, wine stimulates the metabolism, which, as well as HDL, helps reduce surplus fat. So white wine can improve your figure. That is, if you are healthy and eat accordingly.

A History of Wine in White

600 BC

During this period the Greeks dominate the wine market. Wine from Lesbos is much in demand. Its grapes dry in the sun and yield a honey-sweet, gold-colored essence. For centuries, sweet southern wines are the top favorite of wine drinkers.

275 AD

Trier becomes the seat of the Roman emperor. It is believed that the Romans at this time have already developed winegrowing along the Moselle as they have elsewhere along their northern borders. This results in a new, more acid wine style which gains popularity in northern Europe.

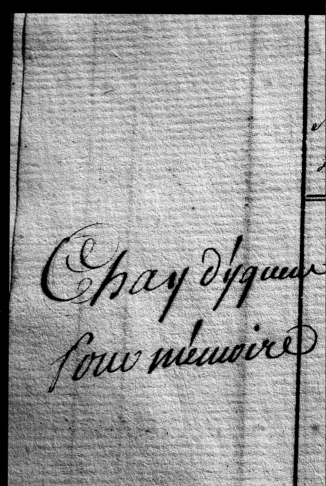

An old cellar book from Château d'Yquem, Sauternes.

& Gold

1540

This vintage of the century produces a Würzburger *Stein* that will still taste superb even 420 years later. It is the era in which Riesling wines begin to dominate.

1953

Former ambassador James D. Zellerbach plants his country estate in California's Sonoma with Chardonnay vines. From the first harvest on, he ferments the juice in barriques. His white *Hanzell* opens totally new perspectives, not only for American winemakers.

2039

Following a lively debate, the Wine Supreme Court makes a controversial decision to once again allow the ancient biodynamician Nicolas Joly to label the product *Coulée de Serrant* as wine. It comes from a 900 year-old vineyard near Angers where grapes are grown in living earth and their juice is fermented with natural yeast. Representatives of the Wine Hygiene Institute have announced to appeal the decision.

The *Kiedricher Berg* vintage 1893 gives proof to the enormous maturation potential of Rieslings.

WHITE >>

Blue Nun is not a very contemplative character. Quite the contrary, she searches and finds friends effortlessly, especially in Great Britain where she leads off the medley of "Hocks" – the name derisively given to German wines. They have succeeded in conquering the British supermarket shelves, meter for meter, as the cheapest white wines. Abroad, *Liebfraumilch* and its consorts are considered the worst of what you can do to yourself with the contents of a wine bottle. As sugar-added mass products, they are the unloved witnesses of the post-war era. At that time productivity was the key in winegrowing, as in other segments of agriculture. The lack of quality was disguised by the addition of sweetened grape juice *(Süßreserve)*. For many consumers, this was the only wine they could afford – at least until their headaches taught them a lesson. As a consolation there were dry alternatives from Italy. These were water-clear, if not diluted with water. Frascati enjoyed its great moment. For years it could maintain its position as the most common white wine. By now, Frascati has been replaced by Pinot Grigio. It celebrates perfect success despite, or because, it avoids exposing its consumers to the taste of wine. For a while *Edelzwicker* (German for "noble pincher") also managed to ride the dry wave until even the very last tippler discovered that it really does *pinch!*

Meanwhile, in the U.S.A., Chablis triumphed with a famous name, under which everything was sold that was transparent and liquid and came from the Central Valley. Thus, the number of those who enjoy white wine has steadily grown during the last 50 years. Technology has increasingly moved into vineyards and wineries. And Chardonnay has begun its rise to triumph. It offers the advantage of always tasting the same, regardless from which continent it originates.

White and Mysterious

Did you know that white wine doesn't necessarily have to come from white grapes? Because the pigment is in the skin rather than in the pulp, white wine, which is usually pressed immediately, retains its light color even if red grapes are used. The best known example is the Blanc de Noir champagne, which is made of Pinot Noir grapes, or Gewürztraminer made of grapes that are reddish gray. White grapes are seldom crushed, so the tannins remain in the skin. Unfortunately, that also goes for a lot of aroma substances so that a great deal of what white wine grapes possess by nature never reaches the wine. Luckily, there are many types of white grapes in which the flavors exist not only in the skin but also in the pulp. Riesling and Gewürztraminer are among them, along with aromatic

Muscats. This also applies to Chardonnay and Sauvignon, although in these varieties it is less apparent. In any case, the pulp is without doubt of greatest importance in white varieties. It consists of large cells that quickly burst and release the juice, which is made up largely of sugar – except for approximately 75% water. In addition, the organic acids play an important role in white wine; among them, tartaric acid is especially apparent. In white wine, the relationship between sugar and acid is a most exciting aspect and results in a far broader palette of different wine styles than is the case with red wine.

Lightweights
Heavyweights

Categories of

Slender
like one of the lighter, fruity Rieslings with good acidity and a certain crispness. A vigorous white, a sparkling aperitif and an ideal partner for freshwater fish. Those from Mosel-Saar-Ruwer are incomparable.

Thin and flat
describes many neutral, although pleasant white wines. Italian and Mediterranean wines are at the top of this category. Müller-Thurgau, Muscadet and South African Chenin join ranks and are decent but boring.

Slim and racy
are white wines that convince with their finesse and balance. Sancerre, the best Sauvignons from Bordeaux or New Zealand are among these, along with successful Veltliners and Albariños, Loire-Chenins and classic Rieslings.

White Wine

Well built

are many whites made of especially flavorful grape varietals like Gewürztraminer, Viognier or Muscat. Often they combine luster and volume with impulsive floral or fruity flavors. These are specialties in white.

Full figure

Great white wines have to possess a well-structured body. They are fermented in barriques and combine roundness, spice and length. Such are the best Chardonnays from Burgundy and the New World.

Heavy

is how they spread over the tongue, these overripe and oaky alcoholic beverages that many Australians, Chileans and Americans celebrate as the peak of white wine. Mostly they are Chardonnays, and they are guaranteed to be filling.

White Wine for the Contemplative

The well-cooled juice of the grape slips down the throat almost effortlessly. But many white wine friends, who lack the time to enjoy, will inevitably find access to the magic world of white wine difficult because there they will encounter characters who at first seem unattainable: their sweetness draws a line. In this magic world, vintners, searching for the ultimate expression that vine, vineyard and nature can produce, are not afraid of facing any risk in order to bring grapes from their best locations to super-maturity. Now and then, they are rewarded with enchanting concentrations of flavor and sugar. The queen of all good fairies of sweet wine serves *Eiswein.* Protected by sheets of plastic from undesirable nibblers and the disturbing effects of water, the individual grapes shrivel until that magic winter's night when the thermometer falls below minus 8 °C, and the pickers can carefully select the grapes. Whether *Eiswein* or Icewine, *Beerenauslese* (overripe grapes) or *Trockenbeerenauslese* (selected grapes), whether Tokay or Ausbruch, Alsatian *Séléction de Grains Nobles,* Sauternes, Barsac, or Jurançon – all these wines demand attention, leisure and respect. Thus, you should devote yourself to them carefully, following their tempting flavors with all senses wide awake and appreciating the interplay between sugar and acidity. Certainly they go well with *foie gras,* fine blue cheese or elaborate desserts, but ultimately these wines deserve our undivided attention.

The Ideal Apéritif

You will come across white wine wherever people spend a couple of carefree hours together. Whether you are celebrating a special occasion or want to drink a toast to success; be it an informal meeting or a formal invitation,

the hosts always strike the right note with white wine. Served in a thin-stemmed glass, even at first glance, it appears so elegant and promising that you inevitably feel like raising your glass and sampling it.

It is the perfect accompaniment to snacks such as puff pastries, olives or cheese appetizers. It is uninhibited by tomatoes and even tolerates salads and mushrooms. In fact, white wine even goes with pepperonis.

White Wine and Love

"At first, consumption (...) brings only a cheerful and comfortable mood over the person. Further consumption increases these feelings comparatively, makes the drinker relaxed, talkative, even flaunting his knowledge in an amusing way, his natural tendency to gaiety seems doubled and tripled. Finally (...) he believes that everywhere he looks and listens, he sees and hears the most charming things. He then gives his environment further proof of his friendly affection by assuring fidelity, love and reverence. Arriving at the highpoint of the situation, he proceeds to embraces, kisses and vows of a questionable nature. With his last ounce of strength he attempts to speak coherently and then follow comic movements while he is trying to balance his body, which (...) force him to sit down again and then, with good grace, he withdraws into a sweet sleep." *Ferdinand von Heuss, 1906*

TOP 10

2

Sauvignon Blanc is above all aromatic with green, fresh flavors reminding of grass, gooseberries or lime. It is very much in fashion.

1

Chardonnay has, in the meanwhile, conquered the world. For winegrowers it presents few problems and is always pleasant, whether or not it is aged in oak barrels.

3

Riesling is racy. W its fruits, acidity an mineral notes, it is ma ing its way, once aga to the forefront.

4

Pinot Gris (Pinot Grigio, *Grauburgunder*) can be anything from a simple fashion wine all the way to a spicy specialty.

5

Chenin Blanc offers everything from fresh, dry wines to full, extra-sweet wines.

8

Gewürztraminer shimmers golden and gives off the scent of roses and nutmeg. Its interesting qualities are at their best in extra-sweet *Beerenauslese* (overripe) wines.

7

Viognier appeals with its delicious apricot aroma and full body. Lately the wine has been gaining in popularity.

6

Pinot Blanc or *Weißburgunder* is developing great strength and length and is definitely winning territory.

Albariño from Galicia is really a secret tip among white varietals. Its qualities are freshness, elegance and fruit flavors which range from green to exotic. Sémillon is totally different. Noble rot *(botrytis cinerea)* imparts a complexity combined with notes of honey and wax. Another specialty is Roussane from the northern Rhône. Finesse, length and longevity are among its positive characteristics. Aligoté from Burgundy, with its spice and dry freshness, is fun to drink.

9

Silvaner is neutral in taste, but from ideal locations it is pleasantly dry and possesses remarkable body.

10

Muscat, often appears as an oily, sweet wine, but when it is dry it is exciting and very intense.

Where White Wine Thrives

A number of white grape varietals tolerate cold and damp much better than red varieties. That is why they occupy the climatic fringes of winegrowing regions. The low average annual temperatures are between 15° and 20°Celsius and the time it takes to reach ripeness is extended, which lends the wines an especially intense flavor. At the same time, higher levels of acidity guarantee the wines keep longer and have a conspicuously fresher character. In such regions Riesling is brilliant, but Chardonnay can also ripen to create an inimitable impression. For example, in Chablis, where the grapevines often have to be iced over in the spring to protect them against frost damage, or Sauvignon in New Zealand, relatively close to the Antarctic. When white grapevines are grown in very hot regions, the wines are often heavy and fat and tend to oxidize quickly on account of the low acidity. That's why connoisseurs prefer whites from cooler regions.

Biological and biodynamic cultivation

It is no accident that winemakers have begun to revise their thinking, especially in those regions where, on account of extreme dampness, they are confronted with fungal diseases such as downy and powdery mildew or rot. Too often they have had to resort to chemical means without achieving satisfactory results. Their search for alternatives has been rewarded by ecologically sound methods.

By improving the soil, not only through compost but often by planting grass, balancing humidity and consciously reducing yields, winemakers strengthen the vine shoots instead of overtaxing them. Many vintners go still further. They respect the cycle of the grapevines and strengthen the natural immune defense of their (precious) plants through application of homeopathically supported substances. Today it is clear such methods that abstain from chemical herbicides, fungicides and pesticides, are definitely raising the wine's quality.

White Grape

still green, not completely ripe

infected by noble rot

Beerenauslese (overripe) quality

Winegrowers who harvest white grapes can be divided into two categories: those who are in a hurry, and those who possess the patience of angels. Still others start out with haste, then wait. When concentrating on dry white wines, the vintner aims for optimal ripeness in which potential alcohol, acidity and aromatic expressiveness are optimally balanced. At this stage he gathers the grapes quickly. It's quite a

Harvest

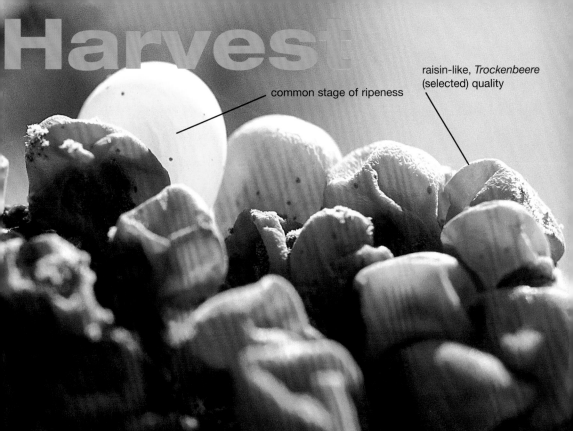

common stage of ripeness

raisin-like, *Trockenbeere* (selected) quality

different story in regions where semi-sweet or extra-sweet wines are produced. There one strives for super maturation. Depending on the traditions of the growing region and the climatic conditions of any given year, winemakers try to delay the harvest. Where nature helps out with morning dampness followed by the sun, the famous noble rot Botrytis cinerea develops. This fungus causes the grapes to lose water and thereby increases their sugar content. In many regions the harvesters go through the vineyards repeatedly to gather only those individual grapes affected by noble rot. The later each gathering, the higher the sugar content of the grapes. In the case of Eiswein, winemakers wait until the frost has frozen the water in the grapes, so that only its extremely sugary juice is released during pressing.

Skin Contact and

In contrast to red wine where one tries to extract a maximum of color, flavor and tannins from the skin through maceration, white wine grapes are customarily pressed as soon as the harvest arrives at the cellar. Since it became known that the highest concentration of flavor is in the skins, winemakers have been racking their brains to find a method that also allows maceration in white wine production. The solution: the crushed grapes are chilled in order to prevent the onset of fermentation. Then the must can be left with the solid material to allow aroma constituents to be released. Through this pre-fermentation maceration, internationally known as "skin contact," it has become pos-

sible to increase the flavor conside ably. This is important for those whit that are finished in the vat and a drunk young. This method gives ev neutral varieties a bit of pep. Ma winemakers prefer crushing the whc grape cluster. In this method grap are not removed from the stem ar stalk and arrive in the crusher undar aged. Pressing is crucial to the quali of white wine. It must be done gently as possible in order to avo a "stalky" aftertaste. At the san time, as much as possible shou be extracted from the grape to gi the wine its character and structu Nowadays, this is possible through t gentle and precise operation of t pneumatic bladder press.

Pressing

Tank or Barrique

The making of white wine always begins with pre-clarification because after the pressing the must contains particles and bits of leaves, stalks or skins – occasionally even clumps of earth. They have to be removed in order not to influence the eventual taste of the wine. For this reason the chilled must remains in the tank for 12 to 24 hours, during which the contaminants settle to the bottom and the clear supernatant liquid can be decanted off. Now the fermentation can begin.

The majority of winemakers nowadays settle on neutral and easy to clean tanks, with a preference for stainless steel tanks with integrated temperature controls.
Winemakers either rely on the natural yeast that enters the must from the grape skins, or they add pure yeast cultures. At temperatures between 17° and 20°C the wine needs seven to ten days to ferment. Must can also be fermented in a barrique or other kinds of barrels. In small casks the temperature rarely

reaches dangerous levels. When new wood is used, the wine takes on tannins and flavors from the wood. This increases the wine's longevity and lends it complexity.
By stirring up fine yeast, called *bâtonnage,* the winemaker imparts additional roundness and structure to the wine. In this way it is possible to achieve an exquisite type of wine primarily suited to being served with fine food. Wines fermented in a tank, however, more often retain their varietal character.

That is the Question...

White Gold

Some wines almost look like water. They often come from high yields where the grapes are immediately pressed. Their taste is most often rather neutral.

Very Light Green

Many modern white wines made from grapes gathered at their full ripeness and turned to wine in chilled tanks have this color.

Medium Gold-Yellow

often predicts an intense expression, be it through t ripeness of the grapes use be it through the fermenta in a barrique or through its first ripening in the bottle.

The Spectrum of Whites

Very Light Yellow
characterizes wines from modern processing of grapes from southern regions or from varieties with low acidity.

Straw Yellow
This is the distinct color nuance of whites which show a hint of development despite their youth and are often fuller and more complex.

Dark Amber
All *Spätbeerenauslese* (selected) or *Beerenauslese* (overripe) and old barrique wines glow in this color.

Mahogany
Very old dessert wines take on this fascinating color.

Eternal, Spun
in its Cocoon

Strange as it seems, white wines awaken
the indestructible, deep-rooted idea of
inevitable finiteness among wine lovers.
Thus, they make haste to quickly drink
their Rieslings, Chardonnays, Sauvignons,
Sémillons or whatever their favorite wines
may be – before they slip through their
hands. They can't imagine what they
are missing. Just as not every red wine
is destined for eternity, not every white
wine is transient from the start. Some
keep very well. Good acidity, a minimum
of vigor and strength give white wines
a fair chance of aging. If they also contain
a good deal of residual sugar, then you
have plenty of time.

Retrospective of Château d'Yquem. The oldest
vintage is from 1876; the most recent from 1985.
Of 100 presented vintages, only nine are missing.

Symphony

Good white wine is like a piece of music. The prelude is when you raise the glass to your nose: at first you perceive delicate notes of flowers like acacia, hawthorn or roses. Often a light spicy note plays along if the wine has been fermented in a new oak barrel. When you swivel the glass, stronger chords emerge. Depending on the wine's character, these could be green or ripe fruits like Granny Smith apples, grape-fruits, limes, pears, or melons. Spicy notes waft from the glass: anise, fennel, cinnamon, or vanilla. If butter, honey and nutty notes emerge, the bouquet gains in volume and expression. The dramatic main movement of our symphony begins with the first sip. On the palate the wine proves to be thin or full, raw or smooth, lively or tired. At the same time, the aromatic *leitmotifs* of its bouquet ring out. Finesse and harmony follow. In the finale, fullness, strength and vigor appear once more before the symphony slowly comes to an end.

In the white orchestra of flavors, fruits like apple, gooseberry and pear, spices like vanilla and cinnamon, vegetables like fern and grass, or herbs like mint, balm and fennel ring out together. Now and then, a delicate flower note sounds above them.

Aprikose	abricot	albicocca	albaricoque
aromatisch	aromatique	aromatico	aromático
ausdauernd	persistant	persistente	persistente
ausgewogen	équilibré	equilibrato	equilibrado
(mit) Barrique-Note	boisé	con nota barrique	notas de madera
bleich, sehr hell	pâle	pallido	pálido
buttrig	beurré	burroso	a mantequilla
elegant	élégant	elegante	elegante
Fenchel	fenouil	finocchio	hinojo
floral	floral	floreale	floral
frisch	frais	fresco	fresco
golden	doré	dorato	dorado
grün	vert	verde	verde
Honig	miel	miele	miel
intensiv	intense	intenso	intenso
klar	clair	limpido	claro o limpio
lebendig	vif	vivo	vivo
maderisiert	madérisé	maderizzato	maderizado
mineralisch	minéral	minerale	mineral
Quitte	coing	cotogna	membrillo
rassig	racé	di razza	con clase
(mit) Röstnoten	torréfié	con sentore di tostato	torrefacto
rund, fett	gras	rotondo, pieno	graso
säurehaltig	acide	acidulo	ácido
schwach	faible	corto	débil
süß	doux	dolce	dulce
Vanille	vanille	vaniglia	vainilla
weinig	vineux	vinoso	vinoso
Zitrone	citron	limone	limón

White
Spoken

apricot
aromatic
persistent
well-balanced
oaky
pale
buttery
elegant
fennel
floral
fresh
golden
green
honey
intense
limpid
vivid
maderized
mineral
quince
racy
roasted
rich, fat
with acidity
weak
sweet
vanilla
with good vinosity
lemon

White Wines of the World

"Which white wine may I serve you?"
"Anything but Chardonnay."
Chardonnay has conquered the world
and has risen to number one among
the premiere varieties. The Burgundy
style has found imitators everywhere,
be it mineral-rich Chablis from
steel tanks or luxurious Meursaults
from small wooden casks. Despite
the generally acceptable quality, a
legitimate surfeit has become apparent. What now? The hero is ready
and waiting: Riesling. European winemakers may have cleared the way
by improving the quality enormously,
but the world-wide future trend
was started in Australia. There, every
opportunity is taken to spread the
fame of Riesling – with exceptional
success.

1 Baden, 2 Franconia,
3 Rheingau, 4 Nahe,
5 Mosel-Saar-Ruwer

Germany

Far to the north of the vegetation zone suited to viticulture, Germany has a superb vinegrowing area that possesses outstanding – actually unique – conditions for the production of high quality white wine. The delayed ripening of the grapes, resulting from the climate, imparts a highly aromatic intensity to the wine, supported by a pleasantly lively acidity. Thus it is possible to create convincing wines with a low alcohol content that still keep well. In addition, late to very late harvests yield fine sweet wines of incomparable character and highest quality.
By far the best grape variety in Germany is Riesling. The tragedy of the German winegrowing industry is that winemakers concentrated on mass production of varieties like Müller-Thurgau instead of exploiting the rich quality potential of the wines of Mosel-Saar-Ruwer, central Rhine, Rheingau, Nahe, Rheinhessen, Rheinpfalz (Palatinate), Baden, and Franconia. Today, a new generation of winemakers is producing first class wines.

✗ Per capita consumption:
22.4 liters
✗ Export: 2.1 million hectoliters
✗ Riesling: 20.8%
21,514 hectares vineyards
✗ Müller-Thurgau: 18%
18,609 hectares vineyards
✗ Silvaner: 6.2%
6,422 hectares vineyards
✗ Kerner: 5.8%
6,054 hectares vineyards
✗ Bacchus: 2.9%
2,967 hectares vineyards
✗ Pinot Gris: 2.8%
2,905 hectares vineyards
✗ Pinot Blanc: 2.7%
2,795 hectares vineyards

Austria, Switzerland, Hungary

Austria has blossomed into one of the most interesting wine-producing countries in the world. Shaken up by the glycol scandal of 1985, its winemakers since then are bent on proving that they know how to produce superb wines. They have succeeded, not only with dessert wine specialties from Neusiedlersee or with Rieslings from Wachau, the Kremstal and Kamptal, but also with Welschriesling from Styria and with Grüner Veltliner.

In expensive Switzerland most winemakers have switched to good and high quality wines. Nowhere does one succeed as well with Chasselas as in Waadt, near Geneva, in Wallis, or Neuchâtel.

Tokays (Tokaji) stand for Hungary's wine image. Now – often under the control of foreign investors – the wines are gaining again. Dry Furmints are also beginning to convince consumers. Other regions are still struggling.

Austria

- White varieties: 74.5%
  36,145 hectares vineyards
- Grüner Veltliner: 36%
  17,479 hectares vineyards
- Welschriesling: 8.9%
  4,323 hectares vineyards
- Pinot Blanc: 6%
  2,936 hectares vineyards
- Riesling: 3.4%
  1,643 hectares vineyards

Switzerland

- White varieties: 48%
  7,156 hectares vineyards
- Chasselas: 36.6%
  5,460 hectares vineyards
- Müller-Thurgau: 4.7%
  693 hectares vineyards

1 Waadt, 2 Neuchâtel, 3 Wallis,
4 Styria, 5 Wachau, 6 Kremstal,
7 Kamptal, 8 Neusiedlersee,
9 Tokay

France
Burgundy
Loire
Alsace

- ✘ Per capita consumption:
  58.8 liters
- ✘ Burgundy:
  White varieties: 53.5%
  13,375 hectares vineyards
  943,180 hectares Blanc
  Chardonnay: 48%
  12,000 hectares vineyards
  Aligoté: 5.5%
  1,375 hectares vineyards
- ✘ Alsace:
  White varieties: 92%
  13,570 hectares vineyards
  Riesling: 22.9%
  3,378 hectares vineyards
  Pinot Blanc: 21.5%
  3,171 hectares vineyards
  Gewürztraminer: 18.1%
  2,670 hectares vineyards
  Tokay Pinot Gris: 11.9%
  1,755 hectares vineyards

As far as its origins are concerned, French white wines by no means have to hide behind the red. The Burgundies are still among the best in the world, whether they are from Chablis, Meursault, Puligny- or Chassagne-Montrachet, or Pouilly-Fuissé. Excellent white wines come from Alsace, especially those based on Riesling, Pinot Gris, Muscat, and Gewürztraminer. In terms of class, the wines of Loire are of no lesser quality. In Sancerre and Pouilly-Fumé, exemplary Sauvignons are produced. Otherwise Chenin dominates the great Loire white wines, whether they are dry, semi-sweet or dessert wines, whether Savennières or Vouvrays. Legendary fine sweet wines ripen in Sauternes and Barsac; Graves deliver the best dry wines of Bordeaux. Jurançon, Limoux, Cassis, Condrieu, and the Jura are also respected regions.

1 Jurançon, 2 Limoux, 3 Sauternes,
4 Graves, 5 Muscadet, 6 Savennières,
7 Vouvray, 8 Sancerre, 9 Chablis,
10 Alsace, 11 Burgundy, 12 Condrieu

Italy Soave, Collio, Orvieto

Italy and white wine – most people immediately associate only Pinot Grigio and Frascati with Italy and no other wines. But there are many first-class whites in the northeast, in South Tyrol, in Trentino, and in Friuli. They are made of Chardonnay, Pinot Blanc, Sauvignon, and the local Traminer. At Collio the exciting Ribolla Gialla joins them. Soave comes from Venetia, its Classico region offers whites with a great deal of finesse. Gavi di Gavi has made a name for itself in the Piedmont and Arneis in Roero. Few whites worth noting are found further south, with the exception of the excellent Vin Santo from Tuscany. Only Orvieto Classico from Umbria occasionally reaches top quality. Quite surprisingly Sicily, in the meanwhile, offers a new generation of marvelous *bianchi*.

✘ Per capita consumption:
55.6 liter
✘ South Tyrol:
2,696 hectares vineyards
Pinot Blanc: 20%
Chardonnay: 17%
✘ Trentino:
13,705 hectares vineyards
17,216 vintners
Chardonnay: 30.6%
Müller-Thurgau: 5.3%
✘ Friuli-Giulia-Venezia:
19,171 hectares vineyards
22,485 vintners
✘ Veneto:
80,953 hectares vineyards
113,239 vintners
✘ Umbria:
18,085 hectares vineyards
33,415 vintners
✘ Sicily:
174,547 hectares vineyards
119,943 vintners

1 Orvieto, 2 Roero, 3 Gavi, 4 Trentino,
5 Alto Adige, 6 Friuli-Giulia-Venezia,
7 Soave

Spain
Penedès
Rías Baixas
Rueda

Modern winegrowing began 130 years ago on the Iberian peninsula in Catalonia when the first *Cava* came on the market, bringing white wines to the forefront. The Catalonians have long since proven that they understand not only how to make sparkling wine but also well-balanced still whites. Other regions have a much greater potential for quality wines, especially Galicia. In Rías Baixas on the Atlantic coast the fruity, sparkling Albariño triumphs.

Exciting whites also come from the hinterland, such as Godello. The whites D.O. Rueda, south of Valladolid, where Verdejo and Sauvignon perfectly join, also stand out. Rioja and Navarra, however, until now haven't produced a white worth mentioning.

1 Vinho Verde, 2 Rías Baixas, 3 Rueda,
4 Navarra, 5 Penedès

Bilbao
Valladolid
Saragossa
Barcelona
Madrid
Valencia
Córdoba
Murcia
Seville
Málaga
Gibraltar
Ceuta
Melilla

Spain
✗ Per capita consumption:
38.2 liters
✗ White varieties: 73%
854,100 hectares vineyards
✗ Penedès:
White varieties: 68%
18,360 hectares vineyards
✗ Rías Baixas:
White varieties: 99.7%
1,978 hectares vineyards
Albariño: 96.7%
1,915 hectares vineyards

Portugal
✗ Vinho Verde:
White varieties: 62%
42,000 hectares vineyards

U.S.A.
California, Washington, Oregon

Even though the fashion in the U.S.A., as elsewhere, has swung to reds, many regions offer the best conditions for white grape varieties. On the Pacific coast this is always the case when the ocean tempers the climate. The often cooler Central Coast is excellent for Chardonnays as well as other varieties like Riesling, Pinot Blanc, Sauvignon, Viognier, or Marsanne. The same could be said for Sonoma County with its many planting regions. Chardonnay is everywhere, even though the best-balanced one ripens in Carneros.

The Russian River Valley is known for Sauvignon (called Fumé Blanc) and Gerwürztraminer. Very good Sauvignon also comes from the Clare Valley.

In the Willamette Valley of Oregon, not only Pinot Noir and Chardonnay has been planted, but also Pinot Gris and Pinot Blanc, as well as German varieties, but these are generally decreasing. And in Washington, Chardonnay clearly dominates.

1 Central Coast, 2 Napa, 3 Sonoma,
4 Willamette Valley

✗ Per capita consumption: 8.3 liters
✗ California:
   White varieties pressed: 45%
   1.5 million tons
   Chardonnay: 20%
   650,525 tons
✗ Washington State:
   White varieties: 43%
   4,860 hectares vineyards
   Chardonnay: 24%
   2,689 hectares vineyards
   Riesling: 8% (891 hectares vineyards)
✗ Oregon:
   White varieties: 67%
   Chardonnay: 10.5% (474 hectares)
   Pinot Gris: 13% (594 hectares)

Chile and Argentina

Whether white or red, Chile's growing reputation as a wine nation is based on both colors and its attractive cost effectiveness. The popular varieties, Chardonnay and Sauvignon, are preferred. 20 years ago the cooler regions were discovered, especially the Aconcagua Region north of Santiago and its Casablanca Valley. In the meanwhile, it has become known as an excellent origin of elegant white wine.

Argentineans with their multi-facetted, pre-eminently Mediterranean-influenced heritage have developed and are still developing a far greater spectrum of varieties than other countries in the New World. Even though in white wine they still depend largely on Chardonnay and Sauvignon, exciting Viogniers, Sémillons and Chenins are succeeding. Now winemakers are exploring the higher altitudes in order to produce whites with a more intense flavor and freshness.

Chile
- ✗ Per capita consumption: 18.3 liters
- ✗ 175,000 hectares vineyards (also for Pisco, juice and table grapes)
- ✗ 0.55 billion liters

Argentina
- ✗ Per capita consumption: 40.7 liters
- ✗ 213,000 hectares vineyards
- ✗ 1.6 billion liters

1 Curicó, 2 Maipo, 3 Mendoza

1 Margaret River, 2 Clare Valley, 3 McLaren Valley,
4 Yarra Valley, 5 Hunter Valley, 6 Marlborough,
7 Wellington, 8 Martinborough

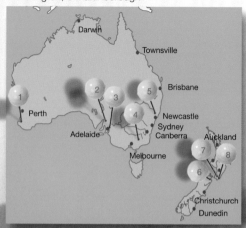

Australia
- ✗ White varieties pressed:
  621,040 tons
- ✗ Chardonnay: 40.6%
  252,166 tons
- ✗ Sémillion: 17%
  105,397 tons

New Zealand
- ✗ White varieties: 70%
  9,557 hectares vineyards
- ✗ Chardonnay: 26%
  3,527 hectares vineyards
- ✗ Sauvignon: 25%
  3,427 hectares vineyards
- ✗ Riesling: 4.3%
  592 hectares vineyards

Australia and New Zealand

In the 1980s Australia astonished Anglo-Saxon consumers with a very volumi-nous, extremely filling Chardonnay that tasted of caramel. But winemakers were quick to learn that this plump style had little future, with the exception of the independent vigorous Sémillon from Hunter Valley. Elsewhere, more balanced, fresher whites are produced. Margaret River, Clare, McLaren, and Yarra Valley are the most famous regions for these. Once New Zealand freed itself from the Müller-Thurgau syndrome in the 1980s, it won international recognition with its grassy exotic Sauvignons. The best come from Marlborough. In terms of volume, Chardonnay also dominates in New Zealand. Exciting whites are, how-ever, possible with Gewürztraminer, Pinot Gris and Riesling. Even late pickings and *botrytised* wines succeed in the cool maritime climate. New Zealand is well-prepared for a renaissance of Riesling.

South Africa

The wine history of South Africa begins with Vin de Constance. None other than the first Governor of the Dutch colony launched this sweet wine made of Muscat à Petits Grains. In 1695, Simon van der Stel's Muscat was among the most desired wines in Europe. To this day the five estates of Constantia enjoy a special status. The Muscat still exists, but today's reputation is based on Sauvignon. It is full of flavor and technically brilliant but unfortunately bears little taste of the earth *(terroir)* it came from. This is true of almost all South African wines. Most common is Chenin, which is usually distilled into brandy. In addition to a few high quality whites, the majority of South Africa's wines succeed not because of their character but by merit of their low price.

- ✗ White varieties: 63%
- ✗ Chenin: 24%
  21,100 hectares vineya
- ✗ Colombard: 13%
  11,072 hectares vineya
- ✗ Chardonnay: 6%
  5,990 hectares vineyar
- ✗ Sauvignon: 6%
  5,758 hectares vineyar
  Alexandriner Muscat
  (White Hanepoot): 3.8%
  3,600 hectares vineyar

1 Constantia, 2 Elginz Walker Bay,
3 Robertson, 4 Tulbagh, 5 Franschhoek

Drinking

Temperature

It is a bad habit throughout the world to serve white wine too cold. When it comes to white wine, innkeepers and waiters are unanimous in thinking of ice. As a consequence the bottles find themselves in the refrigerator, where even a great Burgundy gets the creeps. Hardly ordered, both simple and high quality whites are quickly submerged into a cooler full of ice and stand in danger of losing still further precious degrees. At frigid temperatures, flavor is retarded, just as it unfolds with warmth. Therefore, gather up your courage and free a good white wine from its icy sleep. But consider, the more neutral and trivial the white wine, the colder you can and *should* drink it. After all, it has very little to lose and wins freshness through chilling. Around 6 °C is appropriate. Fine but intense Rieslings and Sauvignons can bear cold but enfold their flavor best between 8 and 10 °C – even 12 °C. White wines that have aged in a barrique generally possess more body but also more tannin. They have earned the right to be handled almost like red wines, especially since chilling accentuates the tannic acid. Depending on their age they present their complex flavors best when served between 12 and 15 °C. Sweet wines with residual sugar should have a temperature according to the occasion. If they are to act as an aperitif, they can easily be served at 8 °C, which reduces the sweetness. If they are served at the table with the starters they can be two to three degrees warmer. When they are served with dessert, they are at their height at 14 °C.

Insert the blades of the opener on both sides between the cork and the bottle neck.

While holding the bottle firmly, press the blades into the bottle up the hilt.

Then you can easily twist out and remove the undamaged cork.

Decanting

Decant white wine? Some waiter will wrinkle his nose arrogantly at the suggestion. The fact is that young white wines, like young red wines, need a lot of oxygen to unfold their flavor. Naturally you would no more decant a Pinot Grigio than you would a Beaujolais Primeur. But when it comes to a really great Graves, a serious Pinot Gris, an exquisite Sauvignon, a Premier or Grand Cru from Chablis or Burgundy, then it is undoubtedly worth making the effort. Besides, this small ceremony accentuates the esteem in which you hold the wine. In addition, great wines generally come to the table too cold. Decanting warms the wine one to two degrees – that can often make an enormous difference in the taste. Especially older dessert wines deserve decanting in order to develop the full complexity of their bouquet. Because of their high concentration they tend to build a deposit at the bottom of the bottle, which is easily disposed of by decanting. And how wonderfully clear is the liquid gold that then flows into the glass!

1

'Glass service' in the
Chinese National Circus.

1 **For young whites**
with simple and subdued expression, this glass, originally from Alsace, has stood the test of time.

2 **The Römer**
is plump and heavy but gives no ground in German country inns and rustic wine bars.

3 **Intense wines**
can easily bear a wide opening but not too high a chimney, so that the flavor quickly reaches the nose.

4 **Dessert wines**
are often served in smaller portions and taste best from these funnel-shaped glasses that bundle the bouquet.

WHICH GLASS FOR WHICH WINE

5 **Refreshing drops**
display their full fruitiness, without developing too much acidity, in this slim goblet.

6 **Barrique wines**
need a large glass with a high chimney in which their multi-faceted scent can unfold in complete harmony.

Why not begin a festive meal with a sparkling white wine as an aperitif? It is stimulating and noticeably lighter than any spirit and prepares the palate gently for the delicate wines that follow. Besides, it is an uncomplicated accompaniment to appetizers. If the starters appear heavy and especially tasty, they demand whites with vigor and character. You are lost if you try to encounter smoked salmon, pâté or filled puff pastries with a lightweight. Here you meet the challenge with an expressive wine, maybe even a semi-sweet or fine sweet wine. Depending on the foods to follow you can then

Dramaturgy

switch over to a mineral or intense wine like Sauvignon or Riesling or a white aged in a barrique. When the cheese is served, it is a pleasure to demonstrate that white wine fits better than red wine, above all a Chablis. For the dessert you can reach into the magic world of *Beerenauslese* (overripe) or *botrytised* specialties that bring the meal to its final high point.

As a *starter,* mussels served with a Riesling *Spätlese*. The *main course* is veal filet, along with an Australian Sémillon aged in a barrique. The *cheese* is Chaource, best with a Chablis – if possible a Premier Cru. For *dessert,* apple tart with an Austrian *Trockenbeerenauslese*.

in White

Melon peppermint punch

1 cantaloupe
1 bunch of fresh peppermint leaves
2 bottles Riesling
1 bottle sparkling wine

Halve the melon and remove the seeds. Make melon balls and place in a punch bowl. Fill with Riesling and plunge some of the peppermint leaves into the liquid. Steep one hour in the refrigerator. Remove the peppermint and fill the bowl with sparkling wine. Decorate with fresh peppermint leaves.

Drinks Made of White Wine

Cold Duck

1 unsprayed lemon
1 bottle Riesling
1 bottle dry sparkling wine

Cut the lemon peel into a thin spiral and place into a glass carafe. Fill with chilled Riesling and steep for 15 minutes. Remove the peel and add chilled sparkling wine.

Sauvignon Cobbler

Ice cubes
0.1 liter Sauvignon
1 cl Cointreau
1 teaspoon lime juice
1 slice of lime

Place ice cubes into a cobbler glass, add wine, liqueur and lime juice. Garnish with a slice of lime.

169.112 years because the Mediterranean has a volume of 4.38 million cubic meters. The actual production of wine is approximately 25.9 cubic kilometers or 25.9 billion liters – and we haven't taken into consideration either evaporation or the thirst of the residents.

Theoretically 14 billion corks, as the pyramid has a volume of 2.6 million cubic meters. Thus ⅝ths of the world's annual wine production. If all the wine were filled in 0.75 liter bottles. In fact, the pyramid is almost completely filled with stone.

The World's Great

How long would all the winemakers in the world have to diligently produce wine in order to fill the Mediterranean?

In principle, 12,811,205,200 bottles, as the moon is 384,400 kilometers distant from the earth. In practice two, three, at the most four, bottles collapse with the slightest breeze.

Wine

How many wine corks fit into the Cheops Pyramid?

Riddles

How many wine bottles would you have to put on top of each other in order to reach the moon?

White Wine as a Stain-Remover

Here is the solution: red wine stains give way to white wine. Generously soak the red wine stain with white wine. Then rinse thoroughly. If you are interested in more methods, take a look into our book on **Red Wine.** Did you know that your Madeira Cake keeps moist if you wrap it in a cloth soaked with wine? We recommend you use a young Riesling or Gewürztraminer because these lend the cake additional aromatic pep.

White Wine Websites

USA
www.demystifying-wine.com
www.winepros.org
www.winecountry.com
www.fetzer.com
www.robertmondavi.com

Australia
www.wineaustralia.com.au
www.bve.com.au

New Zealand
www.wineonline.co.nz
www.nzwine.com
www.cloudybay.co.nz

South Africa
www.wine.com.za
www.wosa.co.za

Germany
www.winepage.de
www.cogsci.ed.ac.uk/~peru/
German_wine.html
www.germanwine.de
www.weinguide.de
www.ecovin.de
www.vdp.de

Austria
www.austrian.wine.co.at

Switzerland
www.wine.ch

Hungary
www.tokaji.hu

France
www.wine-tours-france.com
www.vins-bordeaux.fr
www.vins-graves.com
www.tour-blanche.com
www.chateau-yquem.com
www.vinsdebourgogne.com
www.puligny-montrachet.com.fr
www.interloire.com

Italy
www.agriline.it
www.consorziogavi.com
www.scolca.it
www.planeta.it

Spain
www.jrnet.com/vino
www.doriasbaixas.com
www.perelada.com

Portugal
www.vinhoverde.pt

Chile & Argentina
www.winesofchile.com
www.argentinewines.com

Photo Credits

Most of the photographs that are not individually identified are by Armin Faber and Thomas Pothmann, Düsseldorf.
The exceptions are: 10, Artothek, Weilheim, photo: Ursula Edelmann; 20, dpa – photo archives; 21, dpa – Fotoreport. Maps on pages 49, 51, 53, 55, 57, 59, 61, 62, 65: Rolli Arts, Essen; 78/79 middle: Gabriele Boiselle, Speyer.

Text Sources

26/27: Ferdinand von Heuss, *Videant consules! Eine zeitgemässe agrarisch-medizinische Studie über Winzer und Weingesetz, verfasst im Interesse des durch das Weingesetz dem Untergang geweihten reellen Winzers, des reellen Weinhandels und zum Schutze des Kunsumenten,* 2nd edition, Würzburg 1906, p. 20f. Translated by M. Schroeder.

The publisher would like to thank Elmar M. Lorey for his friendly support.